BURN BOOK

This Book Belongs to:

Made in the USA
Las Vegas, NV
14 October 2024

96831276R00036